DOUBLE VISION

DOUBLE VISION

PHOTO PUZZLES THAT CHALLENGE YOUR ATTENTION TO DETAIL

EDITED BY MEGAN McFARLAND

FALL RIVER PRESS

New York

FALL RIVER PRESS

New York

An Imprint of Sterling Publishing
387 Park Avenue South
New York, NY 10016

Cover art: Comstock Images/Jupiter Images
Additional photo credits appear on page 176.

ISBN 978-1-4549-1102-9

Distributed in Canada by Sterling Publishing
c/o Canadian Manda Group, 165 Dufferin Street
Toronto, Ontario, Canada M6K 3H6
Distributed in the United Kingdom by GMC Distribution Services
Castle Place, 166 High Street, Lewes, East Sussex, England BN7 1XU
Distributed in Australia by Capricorn Link (Australia) Pty. Ltd.
P.O. Box 704, Windsor, NSW 2756, Australia

For information about custom editions, special sales, and premium and corporate purchases,
please contact Sterling Special Sales at 800-805-5489 or specialsales@sterlingpublishing.com.

Manufactured in China

2 4 6 8 10 9 7 5 3 1

www.sterlingpublishing.com

CONTENTS

INTRODUCTION

Opening this book of spot-the-difference puzzles is an invitation to a pre-video game world where images stand still, multitasking is put on hold, and—just maybe—family members turn off the TV to out-"puzzle" each other. It's an analog experience in a digital era, and yes, it's a bit nostalgic—which is why the 100 puzzles in this book are deceptively simple, picture-postcard pretty, and brimming with Americana. (When was the last time you scanned a row of bowling shoes?)

Experts say that puzzles help develop visual perception and act as brain aerobics, keeping your mental abilities sharp as a tack. Tackling puzzles like the ones in this book trains you to focus on fine details, teaches your eyes to scan slowly, and allows your mind to register minute changes. The effect is simultaneously relaxing and taxing, but ultimately, it's just highly entertaining and wildly addicting!

The way it works is simple: On the following pages are two types of puzzles, consisting of either two versions of the same image, placed side by side; or a group of four of the same image. In two-image puzzles, the version on the right is slightly different and has from seven to sixteen changes within. In groups of four images, one of the four is different, with just one change. In the colored bar above each puzzle is the number of changes and where to find the answer key, which begins on page 160.

Puzzles are organized into four levels of difficulty, but don't be fooled! Some images in the "Observant" section may have one change that is maddeningly difficult to spot. And while the more challenging puzzles usually have more numerous and compact detail, a rookie with, say, an eye toward architectural detail or a penchant for spotting faces in a crowd might well conquer some puzzles fit for a Clairvoyant!

For first-time puzzle solvers, however, a few hints are in order. Spotting the differences in any of these pictures depends on many things, like whether the elements in the picture fall into a natural grid (such as apartment windows or items on shelves), the complexity of the patterns, the sizes and colors of the objects changed (bigger and brighter objects are easier to spot, as any good hunter or parent knows), and how many changes affect numbers and letters—most of us these days seem programmed to notice a misspelled word before we do a few more leaves on a tree branch.

In the answer key, rows are counted from top to bottom, and columns from left to right. For example, "the first shoe in the fourth row" refers to the shoe in the farthest column to the left, and four rows down from the top. Where possible, the first row is referred to as the "top row" and the last row as the "bottom row." References to "right" and "left" refer to the way the pictures are viewed by the reader, not what's in the picture itself. For example, "the flower to the left of the tree" means the flower is visible to the reader's left.

Your challenge is to take a stab at these puzzles without consulting the answer key after the first 30 seconds! Remember, no one is going to pull the plug; the batteries won't run out. On the contrary, working out with *Double Vision* may add extra life to your brain and an extra dose of fun to your life.

18 OBSERVANT

10 CHANGES
ANSWERS p162

18 | 1. The clouds are whiter and have changed shape. 2. The wind is picking up: there's a new whitecap on the water. 3. An orange safety cone has appeared at the foot of the stairs. 4. Two bolts are missing from the deck under the railing. 5. Someone caught a fish and hung it up on the railing! 6. There's a new "first aid" sign on the wall next to the window. 7. The word "RIP" at the top of the sign was removed—all kinds of currents apply here. 8. The "S" in "8 ST" at far right changed to "F." 9. The gold striped panel at bottom right lost its gold color. 10. A beach ball has landed on the sand at right.

Here is an example of a typical puzzle. There are 10 changes in the picture on the right. If you can't find them, check the answer key to the right.

OBSERVANT

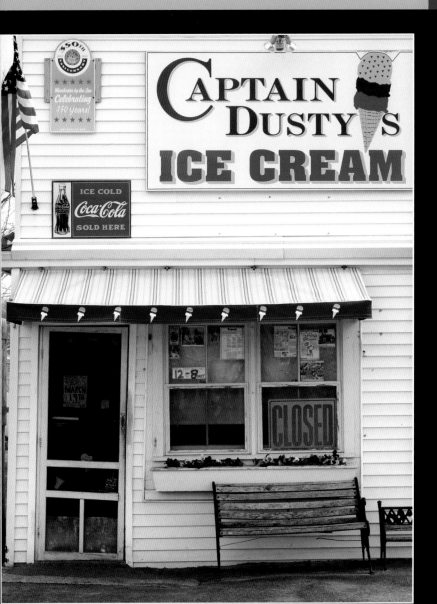

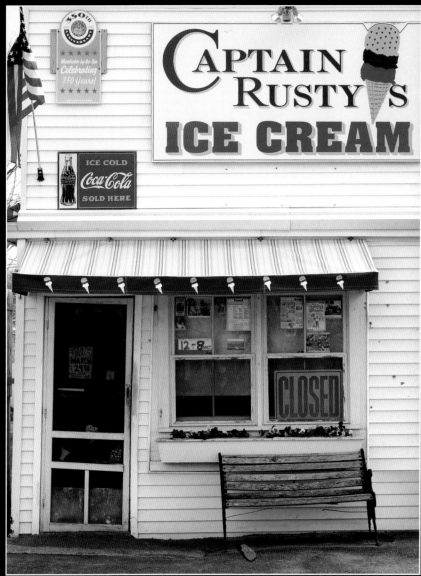

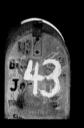

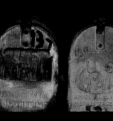
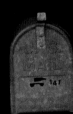

7 CHANGES
ANSWERS p163

PERCEPTIVE

DOUBL

41 PERCEPTIVE

7 CHANGE
ANSWERS p16●

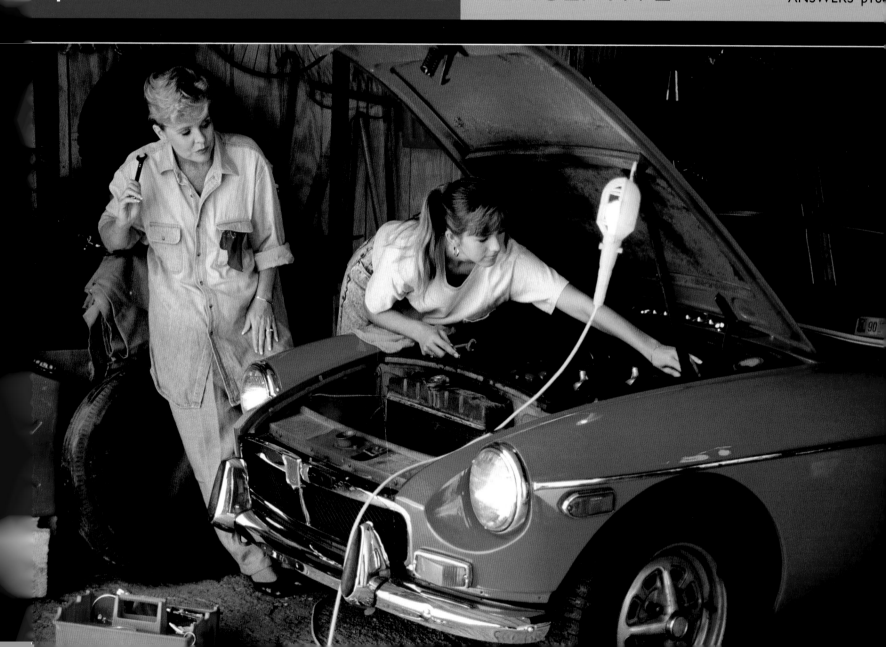

8 CHANGES
ANSWERS p167

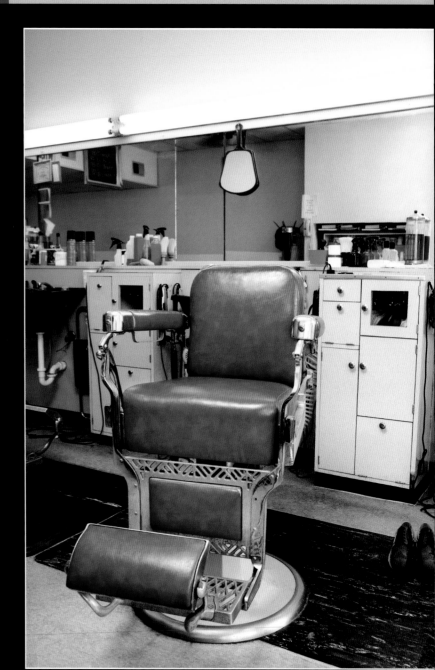

56 PERCEPTIVE

I CHANGE
ANSWER p169

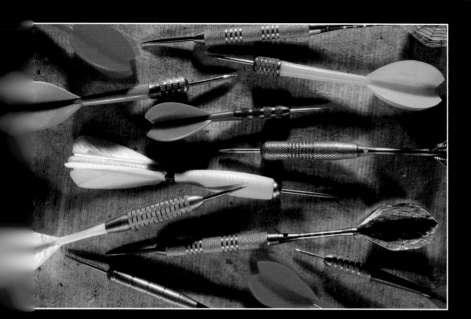
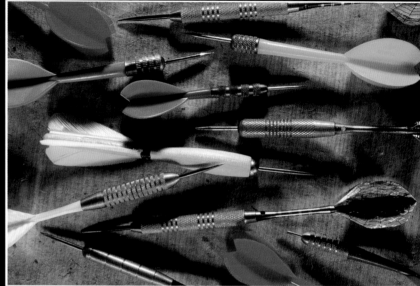
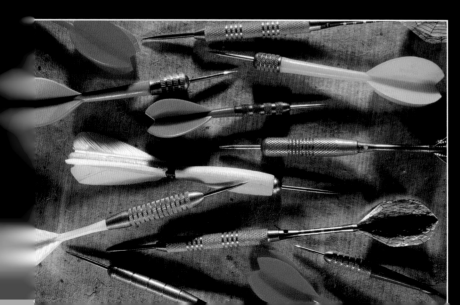
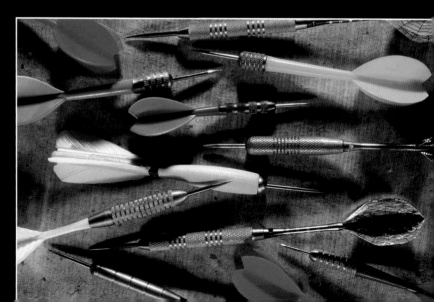

EAGLE-

8 CHANGES
ANSWERS p170

65 EAGLE-EYED

9 CHANGES
ANSWERS p170

CLAIRVOYANT

ANSWERS

1 | 1. The SUV's chassis is now purple. 2. The blue bicycle helmet in the back of the car has vanished. 3. The thermos is now fuchsia. 4. The helmet in the boy's hand is now purple. 5. The girl's tank top is now covering her midriff. 6. The striped duffle has a new color scheme. 7. The black object in the bottom right corner is gone.

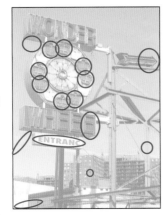

2 | 1 and 2. The windows have each lost a mullion. 3. On the soldier at left, his middle strap now goes over his diagonal sash. 4 and 5. The doorbell has migrated to the right side of the door. 6. The keyhole has disappeared. 7. On the soldier at right, the hat's red jewel is gone. 8. And the pupils of his eyes are now green. 9. The soldier on the left has lost the "V" in his collar.

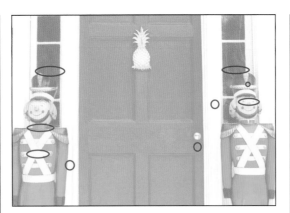

3 | 1. Three more stripes were added to the sign on the left. 2. The flower on the top now has black dots. 3. The "s" is gone: only one frosty milkshake made here! 4. More soap bubbles appear on the right side of the "SOAP" sign. 5. The word "Hours" was painted over on the "Capitol Bread" sign. 6. The licorice in the black sign is no longer trademarked—those red words have disappeared. 7. The two chewing gum signs have shifted—the one behind now peeks out on the left. 8. Some green paint is visible underneath the black, along the upper edge and right corner of the "Coffee" sign.

4 | 1. The black support bar at top left is gone. 2. The wire behind the sign on the left side has vanished. 3. A strand of concertina wire has disappeared from the left side. 4, 5, 6, 7, 8, 9, 10, and 11. The red cars are now navy blue, and the light blue cars are now red. 12. The sign maker replaced the "L" with another "E." 13. The "E" from ENTRANCE has been removed. 14. Someone opened the blinds in a window of the building in the background. 15. The red arrow got longer. 16. The top shadow on the blue pole at right has vanished.

5 | 1. The heel of the first shoe in the third row has turned gray. 2. The shoelace hanging down in the first box, fourth row now has a proper tip. 3. A key has appeared on the front of the shelf at top left. 4. A pink shoelace is now dangling in the fourth box in the top row. 5. The fourth shoe in the bottom row found its mate. 6. A round white sticker is also inside this box. 7. The line under the "8" has disappeared on the heel of the shoe at far right, third row.

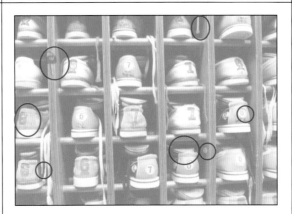

6 | 1. The first kayak on the left turned orange. 2. Extend your trip—a second storage hatch on the third boat has appeared. 3 and 4. The middle strap from boats four and seven are gone. 5. The top plastic cover on boat five is now black. 6. The plastic cover on the sixth boat turned blue. 7. Two rivets were added to the back of the sixth boat. 8. A green kayak replaced the blue one.

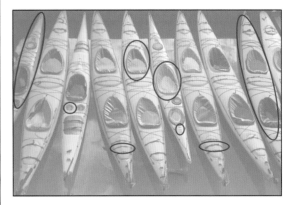

7 | 1. A new spectator has joined the crowd in the upper left corner. 2. The runner at the back of the pack is now number 9. 3. The tiger on the next girl's shorts flipped. 4. The "swoosh" is gone from the red Nike shoe. 5. The ponytail on this same runner is also gone. 6. And her shorts popped another thread. 7. The first-place runner has a ponytail now flapping in the wind. 8. The "1" on her shorts is backward.

8 | 1. The bottom stripe has disappeared from the sleeve visible at far left. 2. The bird on the logo of the pink shirt is flying backward. 3. The "o" in "Palermo" has changed to "a." 4. The "6" on the red shirt at the bottom has lost its outline. 5. The "3" in the top row is now an "8." 6. Someone moved the clip above the blue shirt at bottom right. 7. On this same blue shirt, alpha has become a lambda (or, the "A" has lost its bridge). 8. "Ronaldinho" at bottom right has changed from yellow to white.

9 | 1. The "D" has changed to an "R" on the sign. 2. The cones on the awning are pointing to the left. 3. Someone added another picture in the window. 4. Anyone lose a shoe? It's on the sidewalk at the bottom. 5. More paint is peeling off the exterior wall on the right. 6. The little bench on the right has disappeared.

10 | 1 and 2. The geisha in the first complete column and the amorous couple in the third column have traded places. 3. The cyclist at the bottom of the first column has gotten really big. 4. The dress in the second column turned orange. 5. "MAGGI" in the third column is now red. 6. The label at the bottom of the third column has a bigger bottle and two oranges. 7 and 8. The maid in the top row and the summer strollers in the bottom row have traded places. 9. Who altered the classic Beatles album cover on the right?

11 | 1. The decorative white frame above the window at top left is gone. 2. The yellow stripes on the curtains on the left have faded. 3 and 4. The wooden pole in the foreground, and its shadow on the sidewalk, have vanished. 5. The round hole at the back of the boat is gone. 6. A few eave supports have been removed from the center building. 7. No more TV: the antenna was removed from the roof on the right. 8. Someone opened the shutters on the right. 9. There's a new window display in the shop on the right.

12 | 1. A bone was added on the left. 2. The rubber toy on the left is now yellow. 3. This comb below the food bowl is now longer. 4. The end of the barbell toy on the top lost its orange seams. 5. "CATNIP" is repeated on the bag in the center. 6. A change in diet! The kibble in the bowl on the right is larger and redder. 7. This grooming tool below the bowl grew bigger. 8. A multicolored ball at bottom, below the cat scratching post, lost its color.

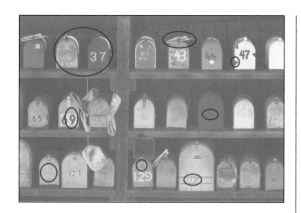

13 | 1. Mailbox 37 and its gray neighbor have switched places. 2. Mailbox 68 became 69. 3. The black label on the second box in the bottom row is gone. 4. The colored circle on mailbox 129 is now complete. 5. Number 43: You've got mail (on top)! 6. Number 47 added a black triangle. 7. The white number has disappeared from the black mailbox in the middle row. 8. A "1" was added to the address on the big mailbox in the bottom row.

14 | 1. The curtains in the first column, second row are now green, and closed. 2. The shades in the second column, fifth row were painted turquoise. 3. The curtain in the window below fell off its rod. 4. The resident of an apartment in the bottom row added fuchsia drapes. 5. Someone drew the curtains in the third column, fourth row— nap time! 6. The horizontal and vertical mullions are gone from the window in the third column, seventh row. 7. The louvers were removed from the third window in the fourth (thin) column, and added to the one below it. 8. The resident in the apartment at the top of the fifth column rearranged the objects behind the louvered panes. 9. The superintendent boarded up the fifth window in the far right column. 10. In the fifth column, sixth row, the man on the left finished his laundry and closed the blinds; now the man in the apartment to his right is doing his laundry.

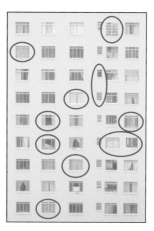

15 | 1. The astronaut bent his right forefinger, and the tip is no longer visible. 2. He now has a mini antenna on his helmet. 3. His face inside the helmet is upside down! 4. The black oval on one of his white canisters is now gray and perforated. 5. A black oval was added to the canister next to it. 6. He can now tell what time it is: there's a watch face on the strap attached to his belt. 7. A few stars on his Stars and Stripes arm patch are missing. 8 and 9. Two black holes on the square white instrument on the right have disappeared. 10. One plus sign on this instrument is now a minus sign. 11. The other plus sign is now an "x."

16 | 1. The sofa arm sports a new throw. 2. The woman's pants are no longer capris. 3. Someone filled her water glass. 4. She's showing her cards. 5. The card on the floor is oriented a different way. 6. The man changed his socks.

17 | 1. Decorative rosettes were added around the bottom of the stair post. 2. A second diagonal-striped parquet border was added to the floor. 3 and 4. The bottom hinges of the door were removed. 5. A bright new red ribbon replaced part of the maroon one on the top of the door frame. 6. The horse and rider in the painting have reversed direction. 7. The pull handles on one of the table drawers are gone. 8. The brass plate has disappeared from the floor in the foreground.

18 | 1. The clouds are whiter and have changed shape. 2. The wind is picking up: there's a new whitecap on the water. 3. An orange safety cone has appeared at the foot of the stairs. 4. Two bolts are missing from the deck under the railing. 5. Someone caught a fish and hung it up on the railing! 6. There's a new "first aid" sign on the wall next to the window. 7. The word "RIP" at the top of the sign was removed—all kinds of currents apply here. 8. The "S" in "8 ST" at far right changed to "F." 9. The gold striped panel at bottom right lost its gold color. 10. A beach ball has landed on the sand at right.

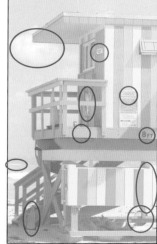

19 | Bottom right picture: The painting on the wall is upside down.

20 | 1. Someone closed the third window on the left, in the top row. 2. The red line on the court is missing. 3. The player on the left is now wearing green sweatpants. 4. Her opponent's shirt changed from red to green. 5. She's also hidden the white drawstring on her sweats. 6. A bolt fell out of the backboard. 7. The right side of the green rectangle on the backboard is missing. 8. The metal plate on the brick wall, anchoring the backboard, is gone.

21 | 1. The attic in the background, at top, and its window are gone. 2 and 3. The shutters on the top right window of the orange building at center are now closed—and so it appears in the water's reflection. 4 and 5. The top window on the yellow building was remodeled, and its reflection has also changed. 6. The gondola in the foreground is now green. 7. Someone repaired a small hole in the side of the canal in the background. 8. The window on the far right was plastered over.

22 | 1. A branch of holly was added to the hanging candlesticks at left. 2. Someone repositioned the pear and lemon from the right side to the left side of the arrangement. 3. A wood spatula has appeared on the sideboard at left. 4. The bird has really plumped up! 5. The garland of dried fruit is now hanging off the edge of the shelf at far right. 6. Salt and pepper shakers have appeared on the sideboard at far right. 7. Another drawer was added on the bottom right.

23 | 1. The metal bracket on the top of the picnic basket, at far left, is gone. 2. The picnic bench in the background was removed. 3. The loaves in the basket are shorter (someone's been nibbling at the one on the right). 4. The rock on the right got smaller. 5. The wine label grew wider. 6. The shadow has disappeared from the Brie cheese in the center. 7. The label on the cheese under the grapes rubbed off. 8. There's another hole in the Swiss cheese in the foreground.

24 | 1. A new roll is in the can on the floor at far left. 2. More magazines are in the right-hand box on top of the shelf at far left. 3. The photo on the wall has flipped. 4. The fish in the fishbowl got a companion. 5. There is a third metal canister stacked up on the shelf to the right of the fishbowl. 6 and 7. The handle slots on the wicker baskets on the shelf are wider. 8. The handle on the metal box at left has vanished. 9. The handle on the teapot lid has grown taller. 10. The handle slot on the wicker table in the foreground has grown rounder. 11. More flowers were added to the vase on the right.

ANSWERS

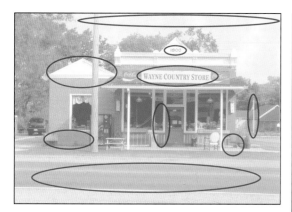

25 | 1. Clouds have appeared in the sky. 2. The building suddenly got older—the date changed by four years. 3. The annex got a new roof. 4. Someone repainted the faded sign. 5. They also got rid of the metal grate on the left. 6. The open green door was removed. 7. A red chair has appeared on the right. 8. Old Glory is no longer at half-mast in the background. 9. The center yellow line on the highway was repainted.

26 | 1. The woman on the left in the yellow shirt has lost the sunglasses from her head. 2. A red flower on top of the picnic basket has turned yellow. 3. The flag in the basket got bigger. 4. The man on the right, in the blue shirt, has dispensed with his watch. 5. One red cup has turned blue. 6. Another red cup has appeared in the front. 7. The woman in the middle on the right side now has a yellow shirt. 8. While this family was eating, someone felled the large tree behind them.

27 | Top right picture: The headlights on the train are now yellow.

28 | Top left picture: A blue flag was added to a pole in the center of the boat in the foreground.

29 | 1. The "T" in "TENZA" has changed to an "E." 2 and 3. The right front and back tires on the left got narrower. 4 and 5. The two red Beck's logos are now blue. 6 and 7. The crane's straps next to the driver's seat have changed color. 8. The lettering on the red front of the car has rotated 180 degrees. 9. The sponsor of the large blue sign in the background no longer has a registered trademark symbol—it's now missing from the logo. 10. The "L" in the orange sign in the background has changed to an "E".

30 | 1 and 2. The red stocking at top left got four embroidered hearts. 3. The green knot from the stocking below it disappeared. 4. The third stocking in the top row exchanged red stripes for green. 5. The red boot at bottom center lost the tiny white leaves on its toe. 6. Three hearts are gone from the stocking in the middle on the top. 7. The small screws on the door at bottom center were removed. 8. The red stripes are now green in the fourth stocking from the right in the top row. 9. The gold heart on the last red stocking in the bottom row, at right, got bigger and flipped. 10. Two flowers are missing from the green stocking at far right in the bottom row.

31 | 1. The word "SERVICES" in the sign at top left has been changed to "SERVICER." 2 and 3. Ticket booths 5 and 7 have switched numbers. 4. Another pendant lamp is hanging from the ceiling in the middle of the picture. 5. The little boy in the foreground, wearing the backpack, is carrying a bouquet of balloons. 6. The last Corinthian column on the right, in the background, has lost a couple of its decorative rows at the top. 7. The arrow on the "VALET PARKING" sign at right is reversed. 8. It's two hours later: 1:34, according to the clock. 9. On the train schedule at far right, "Amtrak" has become "Amtram." 10. A couple of trains were removed from the schedule.

32 | 1. The wall behind the busses was painted. 2. The black plate behind the lights is gone from the bus in the third row, at left. 3. On the bus in the second row, center, the "SCHOOL BUS" sign is outlined in black, and has a yellow background. 4 and 5. A set of yellow lights was removed from the bus in the second row, far right. 6 and 7. And a set was removed from the middle of the bus in the first row, center. 8. The vent has disappeared from the roof of the bus in the foreground. 9. This bus in front also got a new paint job.

33 | 1. Someone added a padlock on the left. 2. The second "P" in "POPCORN" no longer pops. 3. The square shadow disappeared at top, under "ICE CREAM." 4. The double cone is now a single. 5. A white lightbulb replaced the clear one at right, along the roofline. 6. The hotdog now has garnish and a companion dog. 7. The fried shrimp got another lemon wedge. 8. A fourth umbrella now shades the grandstand in the mural on the metal door. 9. The sky on the sign at far right turned purple. 10. According to this sign, fireworks are now on Monday nights.

 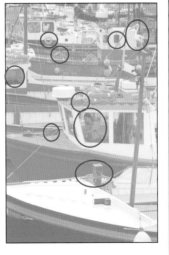

34 | 1 and 2. The vent at the top of the left mailbox has lost some slats. 3 and 4. The holes at the far left and far right in the second row of buzzers have been filled with a screw. 5. The name on the third buzzer in the second row has changed. 6. The word "Rückgebäude" on the left mailbox has lost the umlaut over the "u." 7. The names on the three buzzers in the lower right corner of the left mailbox have shifted to opposite sides of the labels. 8. On the left mailbox, the label on the far right buzzer in the fourth row turned gray. 9. On the right mailbox, an extra "S" was added to the manufacturer's name at the bottom of the black box. 10. An extra vent slat was added to the vent at the top of the right mailbox. 11 and 12. The "Gonsales" buzzer at the bottom of the right mailbox has switched places with the black buzzer to its right. 13. The label on the buzzer in the lower right corner is gone and the buzzer has corroded.

35 | 1. The windowpane on the middle boat, far left, is now tinted. 2. The boat in the background now has a life preserver. 3. A tangle of ropes has appeared in the boat next to it, below the life preserver. 4. Someone left a toolkit on deck on the second boat from the bottom. 5. On this same boat, the black object has disappeared from the red corner unit on the roof. 6. The skipper has returned to this boat. 7. The mooring line is coming untied from the boat in the foreground. 8. Rust is collecting around the window in the fourth boat from the front. 9. A pelican has come to roost on top of the pole in the foreground.

36 | 1. The pea on the far left swelled up. 2. An upside down "5" has appeared toward the top center edge of the bowl. 3. The "H" at the top has a clone right next to it. 4. A "D" lurks under the green bean below the Hs. 5. The chef added more diced potato on the top right. 6. Yet another "H" has snuck in on the far right. 7 and 8. A pair of "J"s has floated to the top on the right side.

37 | 1. The top band is now blue on the top left shoe. 2. The instep has been enlarged on the green shoe on the far left. 3. A band of sequins has appeared on the first blue shoe in the bottom row. 4. The opening has disappeared from the gold shoe in the top row. 5. The tassel of the yellow shoe in the third row now falls behind the pink shoe at the bottom. 6. A shoemaker removed the topstitching from

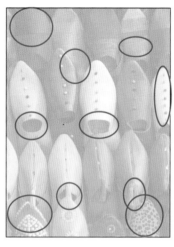

the pink shoe in the second row. 7. A green stripe was added to the shoe at top right. 8. Another tassel was added to the dark blue shoe in the third row. 9. The leopard-shoe has changed its spots. 10. Two more beaded buttons were added to the light blue shoe in the second row, far right.

38 | 1. The cookie on the far left in the back row got a sugar coating. 2. Another small tree cookie is tucked in the center of the box. 3. Someone ate the reindeer cookie at the bottom left corner of the box. 4. The second piece of filigree has disappeared on the box. 5. The tablecloth now has a double stripe. 6. The gold flower toward the top of the box now has an ivory-colored center. 7. One leaf was added to the front of the box. 8. Some of the dried petals on the tablecloth have blown away.

39 | 1. One chimney cap has disappeared. 2. The figurine is missing from its niche on the house at left. 3 and 4. The zig-zag trim on the shutters of the middle house has flipped. 5. Someone lengthened the curtain behind the door in the center. 6. The owner on the right added a window box. 7. Curtains were added to the middle of the top far right window.

40 | 1. The guide's shirt is now orange. 2. A new rafter joined the back row. 3. The whitewater is rising! Check out the middle paddle. 4. The woman on the right in the second row from the front now has a yellow brim on her helmet. 5. The woman in the front row, at right, has managed to put on a white t-shirt. 6. A third boulder has appeared in the back right corner. 7. A salmon is navigating the rapids on the right side.

41 | 1. The woman standing has lowered her wrench. 2. No more yellow cord dragging on the ground. 3. The mechanic bending over has lost her earring. 4. The radiator now has a second cap. 5. A part has disappeared under the hood, at right, next to the hood hinge. 6. The car window is no longer transparent. 7. The number on the windshield sticker on the right side has changed from "90" to "99."

42 | 1. The wood vase at far left grew taller. 2. The couple added a white piggy bank to their collection, on the second shelf from the bottom, at left. 3. The man is wearing a wristband. 4. Someone turned the urn on top to face the opposite direction. 5. A middle shelf was added to the cubby near the floor at center. 6. According to the clock, it's half an

hour later. 7. A new team picture is displayed in the frame in the top right corner. 8. The couple replaced the small black knick-knack on the right with a model vehicle. 9. They also switched the marble and green vases on the right. 10. A floorboard in the right foreground has darkened.

43 | 1. The canisters in the top left cabinet were moved to the left. 2. A brown kitchen towel replaced the green one. 3. The words on the label of the metal can on the bottom shelf now wrap around the top of the can. 4. Someone replaced the

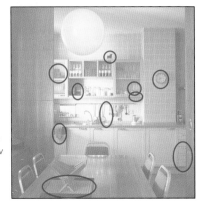

yellow tablemat with a green one. 5. The bull on the top shelf is facing right instead of left. 6. The large ladle in the center is gone. 7. The cabinet on the right is stocked with more glasses. 8. The handle on the far right cabinet is now on the right instead of the left. 9. Time has reversed! It's now 5:15. 10. Three narrow drawers replaced the large one at far right.

44 | 1. Number "4" has disappeared from the sleeve of the player in blue at far left. 2. On the teammate next to him, the label on his helmet is cut off. 3. The strap on the red center helmet has been shortened from the top. 4. A white spot on the red helmet to the right is now gone. 5. Number "5" on number 85's shirt no longer has an outline. 6. The umpire's hat is missing the center stripe. 7. The arrow on the sign in the background, at right, has reversed direction. 8. The rightmost player's shoulder pad is now inside his jersey.

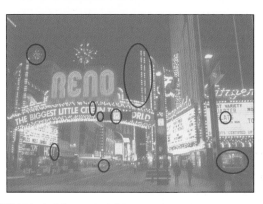

45 | 1. The building on the left has sprouted a lighted starburst on its roof. 2. The illuminated "HOT" sign above the window at far left just got an exclamation point! 3. Has Reno gone French? In the center strip under "RENO," "CITY" is now "CITÉ." 4. The traffic light underneath "CITÉ" turned green. 5. Another car is cruising the strip on the bottom. 6. No right turn: the arrow on the traffic light post, at center, is reversed. 7. A tall strip of vertical lights was added to the right of the RENO sign. 8. "SLOTS" now reads "SLATS" on the marquee at far right. 9. The vitrine display in the bottom right corner has changed.

46 | 1. Writing is visible on the chalkboard at top left. 2. The reflection of the blue spray can on the left has doubled. 3. The two drawers on the left have fused into one. 4 and 5. The ends of the armrests now have rivets. 6 and 7. A bolt from the right side of the chair was moved to the left side of the chair. 8. An extra piece of linoleum is gone from the floor. 9. A piece of the metal footrest is missing. 10. The blue liquid in the glass container on the far right has changed color. 11. The bottom drawer on the right got shorter. 12. Someone left a pair of shoes on the floor at far right.

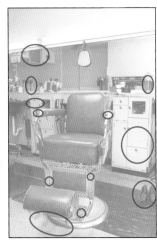

47 | 1. A second outlet was added to the wall at far left. 2. The herb plant on the right has sprung up. 3. The pot rack at top is missing a piece of chain. 4. The dishtowel in the foreground gained a stripe. 5, 6, 7, and 8. The handles on both middle cabinets on the right side of the kitchen moved from the right to the left side. 9. The tomato tile below the cabinets was flipped upside down. 10 and 11. The metal canisters on the shelf of the kitchen island now have labels. 12. Another piece was added to the bowl on the bottom shelf of the island. 13. Someone filled up the toothpick holder on the table at far right.

48 | 1. The sunburst is brighter. 2. A green armband has appeared on the sleeve of the parachuter in the background. 3. This same man now has four fingers. 4. The third parachutist from the left lost his watch. 5. But now we can see his right foot. 6. The parachutist on the right changed his left shoe. 7. A second red symbol was added to his belt pack. 8. The patch near the ear on his helmet is now striped. 9. His helmet also sports another black ray.

ANSWERS

49 | Top right picture: The window frames on the brown house in the back row were painted blue.

50 | 1. A reindeer candelabra has disappeared from the shelf on the wall, at left. 2. The panel under the shelf now has a red tint. 3. A third moose portrait hangs on the wall below the shelf. 4. The trunk on the floor has turned reddish-brown. 5. Two more lucky horseshoes are on the floor in the foreground. 6. A fall foliage garland now decorates the top of the credenza 7. The miniature white pine-tree bench on the middle shelf of the credenza has expanded. 8. A country-bear figurine now rests on the table in the foreground.

51 | 1. The plastic top at far left changed from pink to blue. 2. The little toy animal at top left is now purple. 3. This yellow cap in the center lost its white spot. 4. The word "JUNIOR" was removed from the yellow card box in the foreground. 5. The brown eyes were removed from the upside-down face at center. 6. The top row of the ruler no longer starts with "0." 7. The handle of the orange plastic back scratcher has turned purple. 8. "ACT 1" has disappeared from the black label in the top right corner.

52 | 1. Someone pulled the blind all the way down in the far left window. 2. A star is missing from the Stars and Stripes. 3. "No. 1" has become "No. 11." 4. The red light bulb above the brown sign is now blue. 5. "Truck" now reads "Trunk" on the sign. 6. The red cross and the words "FIRST AID" have migrated to the right side of the white sign. 7 and 8. Small orange lights were added to the top of the truck cab. 9. The small orange light in the center has disappeared. 10. "NONE" above the truck windshield has become "ONE." 11. On the right top of the truck, a red light has replaced the clear one. 12. The fire hose under the front grille was reversed; it now hangs over the right-hand bumper.

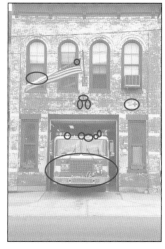

53 | 1. The flowerpot in the window in the top left corner is now green. 2. The yellow square above the window at far left was painted red. 3. Someone retiled under the window in the second column, second row, using smaller squares. 4. The shades were removed from the window in the second column, third row. 5. The top two panes of the window in the third column, third row, are now blue. 6. At the top of the building, another block of decorative tile was added between the existing panels. 7. The white square at top, between the tree branches at right, has been retiled using smaller mosaics. 8. The windowpane at far right was painted green.

54 | 1. The left hand of the player at far left is no longer visible. 2. The goal has been extended on the left. 3. A water tower has sprung up behind the trees in the background. 4. The shadow on the grass at left now has two legs. 5. The goalie's jersey now has one vertical black stripe down the chest instead of two horizontal ones. 6. The player on the right lost the number "1" from his jersey. 7. He added a wristband.

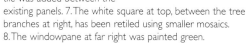

55 | 1. The flagpole mount was moved to the left side of the doorframe. 2. The head of the skeleton hanging from the lamp at left has become a proper skull. 3. This little gypsy now has bangs falling down the left side of her face. 4. The girl in the red dress added a third strand of pearls to her necklace. 5. The pumpkin to the left of the gypsy has become a jack-o'-lantern. 6. Another fall leaf is on the walkway. 7. A flagstone in the foreground was replaced

with a lighter-colored one. 8. A ghost has appeared in the window. 9. The white pot on the step behind the football player is now a basket. 10. The football player is now carrying a football.

56 | 1. The tide has risen, covering more of the pier pilings. 2. The top layer of the umbrella at far left got bigger. 3. The woman in the blue and white bikini at the shoreline has vanished. 4. Another bikini-clad woman is visible above the center umbrella. 5. That umbrella has gained one band of blue stripes. 6. A new bather is half-submerged in the water at right. 7. The blue stripe on the far right of the umbrella at right is now purple. 8. One of the cans on top of the cooler has disappeared.

57 | 1. The father's receding hairline has receded even further. 2. More buttons were added to his shirtfront. 3. He's chopped more potatoes. 4. The glasses and the cups on the middle shelf have switched places. 5. This girl now has two pigtails instead of one. 6. The mixing bowl has blue stripes around its rim. 7. The overhead cabinets above the range hood now have glass panes. 8. They've remodeled the opening directly above the range hood.

58 | Top right picture: This dart tip broke off.

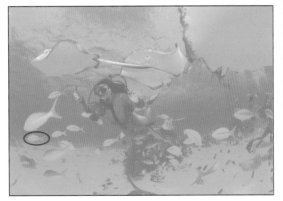

59 | Top left picture: There is now a small striped fish under the large one at far left.

60 | 1. The word "GASOLINES" on the sign at far left has lost the last "S." 2. On the second pump from the left, the word "Ethyl" is misspelled. 3. On the third pump, a metal bracket was removed on the bottom right. 4. Someone deleted the price from the "Hub & Axle Grease" sign on the post at left. 5. On the green pump, a "Sky Chief" sign now fills in the empty window at top. 6. On the fifth pump, a light bulb was removed at the top. 7. A light bulb has also vanished from the Mobil gas pump next to it. 8. The Mobil gas sign at the bottom of this pump has grown.

61 | 1. The intersection got a second street light. 2. Another TV antenna was installed on the roof at left. 3. The arrow on the street sign at left is now pointing in the opposite direction. 4. A square of yellow and brown paneling was added to the facade facing left. 5. This traffic light now has a fourth light. 6. The vertical "Pizza" lettering was removed from the end of the sign on the pizzeria. 7. Someone is sitting on the bench at right. 8. There's a new manhole in the street. 9. One of the wires above the traffic light has vanished.

62 | 1. The gingerbread snowman at left lost his red nose. 2. On the snowman to his right, the red ornaments on the Christmas tree have moved—and there are two more of them. 3. Four white dots inside the heart above the door have disappeared. 4. A second handle was added to the door. 5. White dots now decorate the chimney bricks. 6. The blue and orange candy drops in the center of the cookies on the roof have traded places. 7. The red mushroom top in the center foreground has another white dot, and the dots have moved. 8. The owl at right lost one of his eyes.

63 | 1. Someone shut the window at far left. 2. The birdhouse was removed next to the stairs at far left. 3. The folk doll in front of the first door on the left has vanished. 4. The top stair at center left has been extended and the stairs reconfigured. 5. The little cobblestone pothole on the left side of the lane was repaired. 6. The blue door in the background no longer has a window. 7. A hitching post was removed at far right.

64 | 1. The vines have grown over the window in the hedge at far left. 2. Flat stone has replaced the ornamental panel on the portico column. 3. A pinnacle was mounted atop the second roof from the left. 4. The chimney pots have disappeared from this roof. 5. Three of the decorative cornerstones were removed from the third wing from the left. 6. This faded cornerstone at the far right side of the manor is now brown. 7. The small opening in the hedge is gone. 8. A bottom window at right now has white gridded mullions.

65 | 1. The bottommost branch fell off the tree in the top left corner. 2. A turtle has climbed onto this boulder at left. 3. A new rock has emerged in the stream in the left foreground. 4. The reflection of the cliff has grown longer. 5. A new tree sprung up on the riverbank. 6. There's something in the water in the foreground. 7. A half-moon is visible in the sky. 8. The river grass on the right has sprouted a new clump. 9. Someone has built a small shelter in the meadow at far right.

66 | 1. The lettering "EWS" has been removed from the bottom of the building at left, behind the flags. 2. The row of red lights inside the building is gone. 3. The circular top of the third flagpole from the left, above the white flag, has disappeared. 4. The flag on the flagpole in the center foreground lost one of its stars. 5. The gold ball atop its flagpole has also vanished. 6. The window just below the tree branch at top right is closed and there is no white curtain visible. 7. The woman in the white blouse in the bottom right corner strolled away. 8. The blue and white flag at far right was replaced by a green, white, and red one.

67 | 1. The soldier in the foreground, at left, has lost a gold stripe on his cuff. 2. Behind him, the decorative fan on the blue hat is smaller. 3. The soldier in the top row, center, popped the two bottom buttons on his coat. 4. This soldier's eyes are green. 5. The fourth soldier in the top row now has a baton. 6. On the soldier in the foreground, at right, the blue jewels in his crown are now gold. 7. The fellow in the black hat, at far right, lost the bottom row of his teeth. 8. The red ornament in the bottom right corner, behind the soldier's hand, is now blue.

68 | 1. The word "AIR" has disappeared from the top sign. 2. The miner's pack now contains a pickaxe instead of a shovel. 3. The streetlamp is facing the opposite direction. 4. "NOME" has become "GNOME." 5. A shadow has been cast over "SAN." 6. "FL" has been added to "MIAMI." 7. A polar bear is cruising the sidewalk. 8. Someone has changed the hubcap of the car directly behind the sign.

69 | 1. Someone's painted a pig on the transom in the top left corner. 2. This store is no longer "ZAGAT RATED"—the sticker on the door is gone. 3. The mozzarella sign at top is now blue. 4. The pumpkin ravioli sign to the right of the door is pink. 5. The "PORK" is now "FRESH" and the "HAM" is now "ROAST," according to the red sign. 6. The store's mascot has been sampling the goods: he's fattened up. 7. The "COOKED DISHES" sign at top right is now rose-colored. 8. A jar of red peppers at far right has disappeared.

70 | 1. The girl on the left added a row of ruffles to her pink shirt. 2. The toddler's bangs have filled in. 3. Mom took off her watch. 4. The flowers in the blue square on the right side of mom's shirt are now leaning to the right. 5. What happened to the hole in the center of the cake? 6. The little boy on the right added a third flag to his headband. 7. Two more flowers adorn the collar of the dress on the girl at far right. 8. The coffee in the foreground has become café au lait.

71 | 1. The wood panel behind the rafter at far left has disappeared. 2. The wagon wheel at the top shrunk. 3. Someone replaced the missing bark on the "M" in the wood TIMBERS sign. 4. The "E" in this sign is now an "R." 5. Cowboy lingo spoken here: "Evening" has become "Evenin'" on the colored sign. 6. "STEAK" has become "STAKE." 7. This joint has a new phone number visible under "HOUSE." 8. A lamp was mounted to the right of the door at far right. 9. Another sign is visible on the railing at far right.

72 | 1. The cord dangling over the middle of the surfboard on the ceiling is gone. 2. The metal piece on this cymbal has vanished. 3. The drummer's hat is now blue. 4. The metal drum tip is shorter. 5. The scooter's kickstand is gone. 6. The corner of the box behind the guitarist is no longer visible. 7. There are fewer tuners on the guitar's head. 8. Two missing knobs on the amplifier have been replaced.

73 | 1. The chimney in the background, far left, has grown taller. 2. The window shutters in the background, far left, were repainted in yellow. 3. The wooden pole on the left side of the laundry line has vanished. 4. One of the red clothespins is now yellow. 5. The geraniums in the window have really shot up! 6. Somebody retrieved their bra from the clothesline on the left. 7. The black pant legs on the left got shorter. 8. Someone rolled the blind up a bit on the right. 9. The smaller white pillowcase on the right now has stripes.

74 | 1. The white piece of furniture at far left has disappeared. 2. There are more military stripes on the sleeve of the bomber jacket hanging in back. 3. The orange and red necklaces hanging off the trunk have shrunk. 4. The football in the foreground lost its white stripe. 5. The single 45 with the red label in the foreground is gone. 6. The little coquette has lowered her hem. 7. Someone tossed out the white shoes on the floor at center. 8. The red bowling ball at far right is now number 7.

75 | 1. The wooden crate on the top shelf on the left side has even more holes. 2. An axe has been added to the rack at far left. 3. The lantern is hanging upside down. 4. "LARSON" on one of the crates on the floor has dropped the "L." 5. The front half of the crate top on the floor in the foreground is caving in. 6. Another strap is hanging from the second trunk on the top shelf. 7. More horseshoes are collected on the bench. 8. There's a new tool propped against the wall under the horseshoes. 9. The crate in the top right-hand corner was fitted with six vertical instead of three horizontal slats. 10. The shovel hanging at far right got shorter.

76 | 1. The small balloon in the center has floated into the wild blue yonder. 2. The dark blue band on the balloon on the ground at left is now green. 3. The bottom right panels on the large balloon have changed from yellow to blue. 4. The tree balloon has lost its basket. 5. Another tiny balloon has appeared in the sky below the tree balloon. 6. The man in the white and red striped shirt has lost his shadow. 7. The large gold balloon panel on the right is now orange. 8. The stripes on the man's shirt at right are now green.

77 | 1. The small orange light on the truck's hood at far left has disappeared. 2. A brown hound now occupies the bed of the blue truck in the back. 3. The large red light on the truck's hood is now blue. 4. The flyer in the truck window now features a picture. 5. A fifth bolt was added to the front hubcap. 6. The white trim behind the front wheel has a third "leaf." 7. "No. 1" on the truck door now reads "No. 11." 8. A second metal piece was added to the side of the truck, in front of the hoses. 9. The top hose on the side of the truck is longer. 10. The circular red column at the rear of the running board got taller. 11. The lamppost is no longer visible in the background.

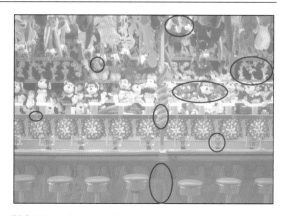

78 | 1. The red number "3" on the purple shelf, at left, has become an "8." 2. The white teddy bear on the middle shelf has lost his eye, nose, and mouth. 3. A new white bear in camouflage has filled in the gap at top center. 4. The stuffed snake on the pole has grown longer. 5. A green decoration was added to the wall at center, behind the stools. 6. The yellow frogs on the lower shelf have turned green. 7. The number "9" above the stool at far right has changed to number "5." 8. Black-and-white cows have replaced the Scooby Doos at far right.

79 | 1 and 2. Now there are snowy peaks to ski on in the background. 3. A wreath was added to the lodge. 4. More skiers have appeared. 5. The skier in the black pants and red sleeves at center has vanished. 6. The man in the yellow jacket toward the front is now carrying a first aid kit. 7. The trim on the lamps on the yellow building was repainted a brighter red. 8. Four new skiers are joining the crowd on the right.

80 | 1. The price of the first sneaker in the fourth row went down to $50. 2. The small rectangular logo on the yellow shoe in the second row has disappeared. 3. The second shoe in the fourth row lost one of its red stripes. 4. On the third shoe in the eighth row, the darker, fin-like element on the light gray toe guard is gone. 5. A yellow star price tag on the top shelf fell off. 6. The black shoe in the third row no longer has small ventilation holes. 7. One of the front stripes on the shoe in the sixth row got much shorter. 8. The red shoe in the seventh row has turned blue.

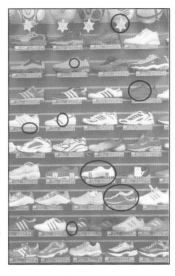

81 | Bottom left picture: The curved fist on one of the tall arms in the very back row, toward the right, pulled out.

82 | Bottom right picture: The "XX"s on the top Exxon sign have flipped.

83 | Bottom right picture: The tip of a blue tee has appeared in the bottom right corner.

84 | 1. The lampshade is now light brown. 2. A natural wood frame replaced the black one on the table. 3. The drawer is missing its pull handle. 4. The remote disappeared from the left side of the table. 5. One of the pictures in the book on the coffee table has vanished. 6. The end of the curtain rod on the right snapped off. 7. The wood window mullions are gone. 8. The wall is now a uniform color below the window at right. 9. Someone replaced the remote on the right side of the table.

85 | 1. This bicycle fork on the left side lost a couple of labels. 2. The small white spot at the front edge of the middle biker's helmet has vanished. 3. The name on the helmet was shortened. 4. The air valve is missing from the front tire of the bike on the right. 5. The sunglasses on the female rider at right are now blue. 6. There's an extra "E" on the middle biker's sleeve. 7. The ".com" extension on the right biker's shirt is no more. 8. The top part of the logo on her shorts has also disappeared.

86 | 1. Three columns of windows were added to this facade at top left. 2. The water tower has vanished from the white rooftop in the center. 3. A small brick structure now appears on the roof just to the right and below it. 4. A long shadow is visible on a roof at top right. 5. Now we know why: this building lost its penthouse floor. 6. A roof at right center is getting crowded: a rectangular structure was added. 7. A red pitched roof now graces the rooftop apartment at bottom center. 8. There's a second yellow cab down in the street. 9. In the top right corner, two more black square structures were added to the roof.

87 | 1. The church at far left now has more windows. 2. The second building in the foreground lost its small chimney. 3. On this same building, the light-colored wood planks above the door have all turned dark. 4. The small yellow building in the background, at center, has another hole in the roof. 5. The doors of the large two-story barn in the center are now closed. 6. The building to the right of the barn has a second window. 7. A second rusty barrel is visible in the grassy field in the foreground. 8. The window on the left side of one of the low blue buildings in the background has moved to the center. 9. The light-blue rectangular object on the roof of the large blue building in the background has disappeared.

88 | 1. Another tree trunk is visible in the background. 2. The plain end of the wood crate at the top of the triangular stack now has slats to match the rest. 3. There's a deer in the woods. 4. The orange buoy has shrunk. 5. A couple of roof shingles were replaced with light-colored ones. 6. The reflection of the boat's motor has disappeared. 7. The chimney is gone. 8. More floaters are hanging on the fence. 9. Look at the size of that fish in the lake at bottom right!

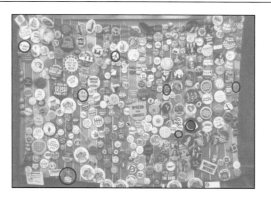

89 | 1. The word "SAVE" has moved on a button in the second column, in the top left corner. 2. A large Darth Vader button replaced the small dark one at bottom left. 3. The yellow "VOICE" button at center left now reads "WE CARE." 4. Someone scratched off the small diagrams inside the peace sign at top. 5. A new black-and-white button has appeared under the Deborah Harry button toward the center. 6. The numbers of the "666" button at bottom center have been changed to a less ominous "696." 7. The CBS button is now a generic eye. 8. A yellow checkerboard button was added in the far right column.

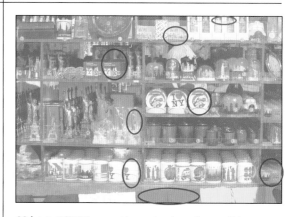

90 | 1. An "I♥NY" mug set has replaced two Statue of Liberty thermometers on the second shelf. 2. A Statue of Liberty on the third shelf on the left side now has a plastic covering. 3. The "I♥NY" mugs are taking over on the bottom shelf. 4. A round price tag fell off the top shelf, toward the center. 5. Instead of a taxi, the white ashtray on the third shelf in the center now sports the Statue of Liberty. 6. The red t-shirt at the bottom is now blue. 7. Two more of the boxed Statue of Liberty figurines on the top shelf are gold. 8. This shelf on the bottom right is now filled with glasses.

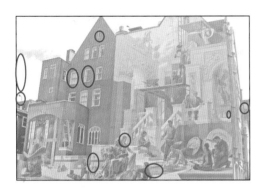

92 | 1 and 2. Red fence panels replaced the blue ones. 3. The cyclist at the left side of the pack, in the middle, has vanished. 4. A new cyclist has appeared in the pack at lower left. 5. Number 171 has changed into a green jersey. 6. A cyclist in a yellow jersey is taking the lead. 7. The cyclist in the red jersey toward the lower right corner now sports a Swiss cross instead of white stripes. 8. The hats on the spectators behind the fence at right are now yellow.

93 | 1. Two lavender dots on a gift bag on the table are now red. 2. A blue dot was plucked from the hat of the boy in the yellow shirt. 3. A wide orange stripe on his shirt has changed to yellow. 4. On the little girl in the purple hat, there is less rick-rack on the front of her collar. 5. The party guest in the red shirt now has a hat. 6. An extra blue flower adorns the lavender gift box. 7. A purple spiral

on the blue gift box is upside down. 8. There's a new tangle of green confetti on the floor.

91 | 1. The crane on the far left is gone. 2. A lamp was installed on the roof at far left. 3. On the building with the pitched roof, the curtains are drawn in the first window in the second row. 4. There's a second dark brick next to the windowsill of the adjacent window. 5. The top vent on the facade is longer. 6. A shovel is propped against the wall to the left of the seated statue. 7. There is a new woman's face behind this statue. 8. A couple of stone panels were removed from the newly laid floor in the center foreground. 9. Another vase was added to the mural on the far right. 10. The window of the building on the far right, in the background, was enlarged.

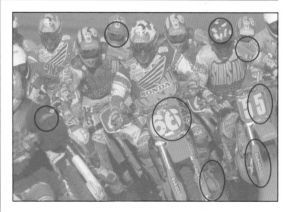

94 | 1. The top left bolt is missing in the bed of the red wheelbarrow at far left. 2. The handle has vanished from the gray door on the left, in back. 3. The typewriter in the left foreground now has an extra row of keys. 4. The mailbox next to it lost its flag. 5. The red letters have disappeared from the green seeder behind the round table. 6. Two new holes were drilled on the right side of the metal sink in front. 7. The tiny black holes on four rows of slats stacked in front of the garage are gone. 8. The tall white contraption on the right no longer has a rectangular opening. 9. The top yellow desk drawer lost a handle. 10. The small slots in the metal spatula on the left side of the table have disappeared.

95 | 1. A third row of shingles in the middle of the green panel above the garage is more visible. 2. The lock on the garage door has been removed. 3. The bushes are obscuring the downspout. 4. Two new leaves have blown onto the driveway. 5. The black drainpipe on the roof at center is gone. 6. The green pediment above the center window has been painted yellow. 7. The four tiny holes in the yellow diamond toward the top have disappeared. 8. A decorative leaf in the yellow pediment above the far right window is gone.

96 | 1. There's a new patch on the black sleeve of the rider in the foreground, at left. 2. The purple visor on the helmet in the back row is now blue. 3. The brake cable on number 66 is loose and drooping to the left. 4. Three yellow splotches on the blue helmet have shifted. 5. The right boot on number 66 is less dusty. 6. The rider at right added a red shoulder guard. 7. His number changed from "54" to "55." 8. Another word from the sponsor: "Dunlop" was added to the fork in the foreground, at right.

ANSWERS

97 | 1. Curtains are now visible in the second-floor window of the first house on the left. 2. Four squares were added under the window on the first floor. 3. On the third house, three new brown squares were painted under the second-floor window. 4, 5, and 6. The hill in the background has vanished. 7. The white spindle on the right side of the third house is gone. 8. The flag and flagpole were removed from a building in the background at right. 9. The slender blue panels under the second-floor windows of the last house on the right were painted white. 10. More flowers are blooming in the foreground, at right.

98 | 1. The teddy bear on the left popped his nose. 2. A second little passenger is about to disembark the plane in the lower left corner. 3. The watering can on top of the microwave is now green. 4. The "0" on the touchpad has become "10." 5. A fourth row of drill heads in the foreground was added. 6. There's no longer a second plastic tie on the blue hose. 7. The football in the middle has more stitching. 8. The photograph in the foreground is reversed. 9. This appliance on the right has one less knob. 10. A tennis ball has appeared behind the racquet. 11. A ball tore right through the racquet strings! 12. More street sweepers populate the painting in the top right corner.

99 | 1. The heart in the top left corner has flipped. 2. The head of a third chicken is visible below the two chickens at top left. 3. The first circle in the row of blue diamond shapes has rotated 180 degrees. 4. There's a seventh white swan in the group of swans at center left. 5. The musician at center bottom has shifted his flute to the left. 6. A second starburst was added to the first star in the top right triangle. 7. Another leaf has popped out on the right branch of the bird-filled tree at top right. 8. The milkmaid at center right has turned to look at you. 9. The red dress of the dancing lady at right is now yellow.

100 | 1. A bracket has appeared on the wall to the right of the metal pipe. 2. The plants to the left of the steps have grown! 3 and 4. The circular and the rectangular iron latticework elements directly above the left door have switched places. 5. The hook at the bottom center of the latticework is now oriented to the left. 6 and 7. Wood "buttons" now decorate the triangular transoms above the windows. 8. The white door handle on the left was replaced. 9. The padlock on the right door is unlocked. 10. Someone restored the missing part of the frame between the two doors. 11. The address is now "222."

PHOTO CREDITS